DONATED BY
THE KENTUCKY BOOK FAIR
WWW.KYBOOKFAIR.COM

"Take time to smell —
Life's Roses!"

Always, *[signature]*

D1203188

THE UNSPOKEN LANGUAGE OF

Fans & Flowers

LINDA J. HAWKINS

Heart to Heart Publishing

Other books by Author Linda J. Hawkins

Alexander and the Great Food Fight

Catering to Children with Recipes for Memorable Tea Parties

Alexander and the Great Vegetable Feud

Alexander Enjoys His Fruits & Vegetables

Alexander's Enrichment Activities

Alexander's Read & Sing-A-Long

Heart to Heart Publishing, Inc.
519 Muddy Creek Road • Morgantown, KY 42261
(270) 526-5589
www.lindajhawkins.com • e-mail: hawkinslindaj@logantele.com

Copyright © 2007 Linda J. Hawkins
Publishing Rights: Heart to Heart Publishing, Inc.
Library of Congress Control No. 2007940415
ISBN 0-9742806-9-0

All rights reserved. No part of this book may be reproduced or utilized in any form or by any means, electronic or mechanical, including photocopying, recording, or by any information storage and retrieval system, without permission in writing. Fax to Permission Request (270) 526-7489.

Editor: Elizabeth Doucet
Co-Editor: Evelyn Byers
Photographer: Barbara Yonts • (270) 821-2683
Layout & Design: Legacy Ink Publishing • E-mail: creative@legacyinkpublishing.com

Printed in U.S.A.

First Edition
1 2 3 4 5 6 7 8 9 10

Notice: Every effort has been made to locate the copyright owners of the material used in this book. Please let us know if an error has been made, and we will make any necessary changes in future printings.

The author or publisher assumes no responsibility for health issues, or subsequent harm that might be an allergy reaction to food or flowers from the use of any of these recipes listed in this book.

Contents

... also that every man should eat and drink, and enjoy the good of all his labour, it is the gift of God.

– Ecclesiastes 3:13

Introduction

Dear Friend,

This gift book was written for children 2-92. The child within never tires of being lovingly spoiled. In this age of rush-rush, hurry-hurry, it is refreshing to slow down and enjoy the love and friendship of those we hold dear. Take the time to play, perhaps with fans or flowers or sharing a tea time together. Most of all, may you laugh and grow closer while sharing this book – from my heart to yours.

– *Linda J. Hawkins*

Adopt the pace of nature,
Her secret is patience.
– Ralph Waldo Emerson (1803-1882)

*There is a time for everything, and a season for every activity under heaven:
a time to be born, and a time to die, a time to plant and a time to uproot...*

– Ecclesiastes 3:1-2

Dedication

This work is dedicated to all branches of the military, the past, the present, and future. May God's richest blessings rest upon each, as you fight, have fought, and continue to fight for the freedom of this great nation.

Our task must be to free ourselves by widening our circle of compassion to embrace all living creatures and the whole of nature in its beauty.

– Author Unknown

Preface

There was once a time when women could sit in the parlor primly savoring a cup of Earl Grey tea, while sharing thoughts that those of the feminine gender could really appreciate. Recreate this era by phoning your friends, inviting them over to chat and enjoy a cup of tea. While visiting—share this book together—plan and look forward to a special event at which ideas from this book can be implemented with love and laughter filling the atmosphere. Allow younger ones to participate in the fun. This book was created for all ages to enjoy.

May I a small house and large garden have; and a few friends, and many books, both true, both wise, and both delightful too!

– Abraham Cowley (1618-1667)

9

History of Fans

Throughout the years, people have expressed their feelings in different forms, verbally, as well as in written words, and by unspoken expression through body language, fan, or flowers.

In Spain during the 1600s, a Spaniard named Fenella wrote a language for fans. Both males and females learned and practiced this form of communication. While they were enjoying a ball or social event, communication could take place without their speaking a word. It was of great importance to know the language of the fan and its unspoken meanings. If you saw someone who interested you, you would signal him or her through silent gestures. Everyone wanted to know exactly what each movement meant—to avoid mistaking the meaning conveyed by the fan. The Spanish, whose social rules were stricter, used the language enthusiastically. France and England also used it with eloquence, though to them, it was merely a harmless diversion to help pass away many a tedious afternoon. Therefore, fans were used for more than cooling oneself.

During and 1700s, young ladies and gentlemen attended classes to learn the language of the fan. Instructions were first published in Spanish, later in German by Fran Bartholomew and finally, Duvelleroy of Paris translated them into English, printing them on small cards.

In the 1800s, a new technique was developed: printing on fans. In 1851, one hundred thirty-five printers were listed in London's post offices. Fans from the Spanish market were of the embossed paper leaf style, decorated with a colored lithograph and mounted on pierced and painted wooden sticks. Many fans today are made of other materials, such as paper or silk, attached to plastic or wooden sticks, like those of previous times. Sandalwood fans were sprayed or soaked with cologne so that with each movement of the fan, a pleasant fragrance permeated the air.

During the 1800s, America's Southern belles used their fans for flirtation. A coy glance from behind a fan would encourage the swain to think he had a chance of winning the lady's heart. A quick flick of the wrist and snap of the fan indicated dismissal of the young man's efforts.

With the advent of almost universal air conditioning, the use of fans has waned. Thanks to modern technology, nobody has trouble communicating face to face or electronically with members of the opposite sex. While this may be an improvement in many cases, it does away with the element of mystery that users of the fan might have delighted in employing.

Why not take a few moments of your leisure time to study the 33 movements of fans? You may even wish to practice them on your admirer. It will add a new element of flirtation to your romance. Or give young ladies fun moments with much laughter at their next tea party, as they indulge in the unspoken language of the fan.

Please have fun learning the thirty-three unspoken movements of the fan. I would have preferred using only positive movements but then Mr. Fenella's history of fans would be incomplete.

Carrying in right hand in front of face means *Follow Me*.

Perfumes are the feelings of flowers.

– Heinrich Heine (1797-1856)

Fanning slowly says *I am married*.

Touching the unfolded fan in the act of waving signifies *I long always to be near thee*.

Open and shut says *You are cruel*.

Covering the left ear with the open fan warns *Do not betray our secret*.

Carrying in left hand, open, says *Come and talk to me*.

Letting it rest on right cheek denotes *Yes*.

Shutting the fully-open fan very slowly says *I promise to marry you*.

*A thing of beauty
is a joy forever.*

– John Keats (1795-1821)

Dropping it means *We will be friends*.

*Grow where you
are planted.*

– Unknown

Drawing across the forehead warns *You have changed*.

Drawing across the cheek indicates *I love you*.

*The dahlia you brought to our isle
Your praises forever shall speak:
Mid gardens as sweet as your smile,
And colour as bright as your cheek.*

– Lord Holland to Lady Webster; early 1800s

With little finger extended bids *Good-bye*.

Presenting a number of sticks, fan partly opened, asks *At what hour*?

Gazing pensively at the shut fan plaintively asks *Why do you misunderstand me?*

Carrying in left hand in front of face signifies *Desirous of acquaintance.*

Roses do comfort the heart.

– *William Langham (1756-1830)*

Fanning quickly signifies *I am engaged.*

21

Drawing across the eyes means *I am sorry*.

I know a bank whereon the wild thyme blows
Where oxlips and the nodding violet grows...

– *William Shakespeare (1564-1616)*, A Midsummer Night's Dream

Open wide means *Wait for me*.

Placed behind head says *Don't forget me*.

Drawing through the hand says *I hate you*.

The shut fan held to the heart delivers encouraging news: *You have won my love.*

With handle to lips commands *Kiss me.*

The shut fan resting on the right eye asks *When may I be allowed to see you?*

Threatening with the fan shut warns *Do not be so imprudent.*

Whether we wake or we sleep,
Whether we carol or weep,
The Sun with his planets
in chime,
Marketh the going of Time.

– Edward Fitzgerald (1809-1883)

If you have a mind at peace, and a heart that cannot harden, go find a door that opens wide upon a lovely garden.

– Author unknown

Pressing the half-open fan to the lips beckons *You may kiss me*.

Carrying in the left hand means *You are too willing*.

Clasping the hands under the open fan says
Forgive me, I pray you.

Letting it rest on left cheek says *No.*

Twirling in the right hand delivers the news *I love another.*

How wonderful it is that nobody need wait a single moment before starting to improve the world.

– Anne Frank (1929-1945)

Presented shut asks *Do you love me?*

Touching tip with finger means *I wish to speak to you.*

Placing it on left ear warns *I wish to get rid of you.*

Twirling in the left hand reminds that *We are being watched.*

God gave us memories, that we might have June roses in the December of our lives.

– *Sir James Matthew Barrie (1860-1937)*

Mares eat oats and does eat oats, And little lambs eat ivy,
Kids eat ivy too, Wouldn't you?

– Mother Goose

Introduction to Flowers

Years after the silent language of fans was documented, the attachment of silent communication and meaning was added for plants, especially roses. The study of such attachment is called "phyllanthography." Lovers sent flowers to speak to the hearts of their dearly- beloved sweethearts. A flutter of excitement would sweep throughout the entire household when flowers were delivered to the door. Questions abounded—What color? Who sent them? What does this mean?

Flowers are all the more eloquent when both the giver and the receiver are aware of their hidden meanings. For the Victorians, the white ranuncule carried the message "I am dazzled by your charms." It also was a symbol of innocence and purity. If the same flower was placed in an entranceway offering a greeting to guests, it was a symbol of a hearty welcome.

One of the most poetic blossoms is from the (syringa vulgaris) lilac bush. Brought to America by early settlers, lilacs became a popular spring-time plant. Each spring brings soft colorful blooms, and as the swaying branches blow gently in the breeze, they release the aroma of the lovely lilac. This is one of my favorites.

In decades past, to celebrate the beginning of the season, young ladies were crowned with lilacs, either purple or white, during festivals. If a maiden wore the flowers on any other day, it was whispered that she would never marry. Today's modern lilacs last much longer than the first two weeks of May. They still have all the aroma of their ancestors, yet with increased disease resistance and hardiness.

The Victorians recognized the splendor of the elegant calla lily, giving it the meaning of "magnificent beauty." Only serious admirers bestowed a bouquet of expensive calla lilies as the ultimate gift of indulgence to that special someone.

> *There is simply the rose; it is perfect in every moment of its existence.*
>
> *– Ralph Waldo Emerson (1803-1882)*

The rose was crowned the Queen of Flowers. Americans have long held a special place in their hearts for roses. It is a symbol of love, devotion, beauty, and eternity. The rose was designated as the National Floral Emblem of the United States in an official proclamation on November 20, 1986. Artists have long been influenced by the grace of the rose. Another meaning of a full-blown rose is secrecy. Confidentiality was a promise given at a meeting if a rose was pinned over the doorway. President Ronald Reagan wrote and signed in Resolution 15, "We find roses throughout our art, music and literature. We decorate our celebrations and parades with roses. Most of all, we present roses to those we love, and we lavish them on our altars, our civil shrines and the final resting place of our honored dead."

The rose, with its silken petals and lovely, blushing shades, stands paramount as the number one symbol of love. Over the decades, roses have been one of the main flowers placed into a lover's hands. It appears that flowers can communicate with eloquence what the heart recognizes. Romantic evenings are begun or topped off with the beauty of lovely blossoms.

The lily of the valley (*convallaria*) has been credited with heightening romance: In ancient times, its delicate perfume was considered to be a love potion and its essential oil was deemed so valuable that it was hidden away and placed in pure gold vessels. Every May in France people can still be found placing lily of the valley's slender stalks in their buttonholes for

special occasions. It is a flower often used in weddings to signify devotion.

Flowers bring joy and delight to givers and receivers. They add to any room or occasion. Their importance as a lovely form of decoration cannot be exaggerated. Whether young or old, male or female, everyone loves to feel wanted, even needed. Beautiful blooms can say, "You are loved, I (we) care. You are very important to me (or us)."

Historically a Victorian bridal bouquet, the tussie-mussie was a popular arrangement that may still be used for any occasion. It is a small, compact cluster of flowers with bound stems, creating an ultra-charming round bouquet. From a dainty fingertip bouquet to a more lavish creation, the tussie-mussie can be designed to be held in the hand or slipped

Interesting Facts about Roses

• George Washington, our first president, was also our first rose breeder.

• The rose is native to the United States. One of the oldest fossilized imprints of a rose was found on a slate deposit in Florissant, Colorado; it is estimated to be 25 million years old.

• There are nearly 900 acres of greenhouse area dedicated to the production of freshly-cut roses in the United States.

• In May, at the famous Kentucky Derby, a garland of roses created by hand-stitching them on a blanket is placed upon the neck of the winning horse. The rose is a fashion "classic" rose. Some refer to it as a "run-for-the-roses."

into a favorite vase. Tussie refers to a knot of flowers, and mussie, or "mossie," refers to the moist earth that keeps the flowers fresh. There were holders made of gold, silver, or brass to hold these dainty flowers, sometimes referred to as a nosegay. Used as centerpieces for a room, they imparted a fresh aroma.

Victorians claimed the herb garden as their dictionary of love. With a tussie-mussie (a bouquet composed of appropriately chosen herbs and flowers) in hand, man or woman could communicate tender thoughts they wouldn't dare speak.

> ## Tips for Making Cut Roses Last Longer:
>
> • Be sure to re-cut the stems if they are not delivered in a vase or container with water. If you do not re-cut the stems, the roses cannot take in water and will likely die within a few hours. Cut the bottom at least ½ inch off at an angle, with a clean knife.
>
> • Use a clean container with clean water. Be sure that any leaves that fall below the water line are removed (leaves in the water promote bacteria, which decreases the longevity of the roses).
>
> • Place roses where they will not be exposed to direct sunlight, drafts, or extreme heat or cold.
>
> • Clean vase every 2 or 3 days with hot soapy water and a small amount of bleach. Rinse. Add fresh water. Re-cut stems as above and enjoy.

Much of the earth's bounty – from endive to mint, burdock to houseleeks, basil to coriander – has been claimed at one time or another to have magical powers of attracting love.

The following herbs, with a central bunch of rosebuds as the motif, may be used in a tussie-mussie for someone you love.

• Ivy for constancy and friendship.
• Marjoram for blushing and happiness.
• Myrtle for love.
• Sage for domestic virtue and immortality.
• Rosebuds for young love.
• Rosemary for remembrance; your presence revives me.
• Rose geranium for preference.
• Statice for everlasting emotions.
• Viola tricolor or Johnny jump-up for thoughts of you, or heartsease.

Borage is a beautiful plant with star-shaped blue flowers. It has a hint of cucumber flavor; the language of flowers says borage is for courage. As the heart needs courage to continue, the garden needs this plant as well. Borage was said not only to bring courage, but also to make everyone happier.

Parsley was used in Rome to honor victorious athletes. It was an important herb for their festivals. It was used to sweeten breath. We now see it used primarily as a garnish in many restaurants.

In Elizabethan times, the language of flowers was well known, and small nosegays, or tussie-mussies, were given to convey lovers' messages. Victorian ladies perfected the art of sending floral messages as an acceptable way of changing social contacts. They planned specialized gardens to grow the flowers or herbs they desired for tussie-mussies. Herb gardens of churches were important for special services and festivals. Houses of worship were decorated with special care, using flowers and sweet-smelling herbs. They were draped over the altar, fastened to the walls, tied to the ends of pews, and even scattered on the floors.

Consider having your own floral language revival, whether it be at your next family meal, lovingly served with herbs and flowers, or a wedding service overflowing with freshly-cut blossoms. The romantic and exotic touch of herbs and flowers feeds the body and refreshes the soul.

Flower Customs

- Deliver a proposal of marriage the Victorian way by giving an armload of irises.

- The three petals of the iris are symbols of faith, wisdom, and valor on the fleur-de-lis, flower of Louis VII of France.

- Because the cattalya orchid means mature charm, it has become the favorite corsage to give on Mother's Day.

- Wearing a corsage over your heart means feelings are mutual.

- Wearing a corsage over your bosom means friendship.

- Wear red or colored flowers if your mother is alive. Wear white _only_ if she is deceased.

- Victorian legend says to include ivy in your bridal bouquet. This ivy should be rooted and planted as a commemoration of your special day.

- When Prince Charles and Princess Diana married, she had myrtle and veronica in her bouquet cut from Queen Victoria's special garden. The original plants were planted from Queen Victoria's tussie-mussie.

*I'm glad the sky is painted blue
And the Earth is painted green
With such a lot of nice fresh air
All sandwiched in between.*

– Unknown

The Unspoken Language Of Flowers

Aloe . . . . Healing

Amaranth . . . . With affection

Amaryllis . . . . Pride

Angelica . . . . Inspiration

Anemone . . . . Unfading love

Apple blossom . . . . Preference

Aspen . . . . Fearlessness

Aster . . . . Variety, afterthought, fidelity, love

Azalea . . . . Temperance, womanhood

Baby's Breath . . . . Pure heart, festivity, gaiety

Basil . . . . Love or hate

Bay . . . . Victory, strength

Bee Balm . . . . Virtue

Beech . . . . Tolerance

Begonia . . . . Beware

Bells-of-Ireland . . . . Whimsy, good luck

Bittersweet . . . . Truth

Bleeding Heart . . . . Love

Bluebell . . . . Constancy

Borage . . . . Bravery

Buttercup . . . . Cheerfulness, riches

Caladium . . . . Great joy and delight

Calendula . . . . Winning grace, joy

Calla Lily, white . . . . . . Sophistication, seduction

Camellia . . . . Perfected loveliness, gratitude

Carnation, pink . . . . . . Maternal love, beauty, pride, mother's undying love

Carnation, red . . . . Deep love

Carnation, light red . . . . Admiration

Carnation, white . . . . . . Symbol of democracy, pure love, good luck

Carnation, yellow . . . . . Fascination or rejection

Carnation, purple . . . . . Capriciousness

Carnation, striped . . . . . Refusal of love

Just living is not enough, said the butterfly. One must have sunshine, freedom, and a little flower.

– Hans Christian Anderson (1805-1875)

35

Cattail . . . . .Peace
Chamomile . . . . .Wisdom, patience
Cherry . . . . .Composure
Chestnut bud . . . . .Readiness to learn
Chicory . . . . .Self-love
Chrysanthemum, white .Truthfulness
Chrysanthemum, red . . .Love
Chrysanthemum, yellow.Cheerfulness or slighted
love
Clematis. . . . . .Mental beauty
Clover, Shamrock . . . . . .Good luck, light-
heartedness
Columbine. . . . . .Resolution
Coriander. . . . . .Lust
Cornflower, ...Delicacy, felicity, unity
Bachelor's Button
Crocus . . . . .Cheerfulness
Cyclamen . . . . .Shyness, modesty
Dahlia . . . . .Good taste
Daisy . . . . .Innocence, simplicity,
gentleness, loyal love

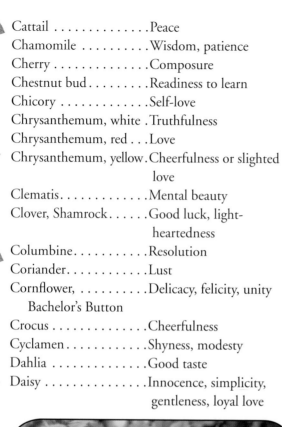

Dandelion . . . . .Wishes come true
Dead leaves . . . . .Sadness
Dill . . . . .Good cheer, survival
Dogwood. . . . . .Durability
Dusty Mile. . . . . .Happiness, industriousness
Elm . . . . .Reliability
Eucalyptus . . . . .Protection
Evergreen bough . . . . . .Everlasting life
Fennel . . . . .Worthy of all praise
Fern, Asparagus . . . . . . .Airy grace
Fern . . . . .Discretion, fascination,
sincerity
Feverfew. . . . . .Good health, warmth,
flirtation, protection
Fir . . . . .Time
Forget-me-not . . . . . . .Remembrance, true love,
good memories
Forsythia . . . . .Anticipation
Foxglove. . . . . .Insincerity
Fuchsia. . . . . .Good taste
Freesia . . . . .Innocence
Gardenia . . . . .Secret love, ecstasy
Geranium, red . . . . . . .Comfort, beauty without
virtue
Geranium, scented . . . . .Happiness
Gladiolus . . . . .Generosity, strength of
character

Goldenrod . . . . .Encouragement, precaution
Grape Hyacinth . . . . . . .Birth
Grass . . . . .Submission
Hawthorne. . . . . .Hope
Heather . . . . .Admiration, wishes come true
Heliotrope . . . . .Faithfulness, devotion
Hemlock . . . . .You will be my death
Hibiscus. . . . . .Delicate beauty
Holly . . . . .Love, friendship, eternal life
Hollyhock . . . . .Ambition
Honeysuckle. . . . . .Devoted affection, bonds of love, generosity
Hyacinth . . . . .Sport, game, play, loveliness
Hydrangea . . . . .Thanks for understanding, boastfulness
Hyssop. . . . . .Deter evil
Iris . . . . .Faith, wisdom and valor, a message for thee
Iris, yellow . . . . .Passion
Ivy . . . . .Wedded love, constancy, trustfulness, fidelity
Jasmine . . . . .Grace, elegance

Long as there's a sun that sets, primroses will have their glory; Long as there are violets, they will have a place in story.

– William Wordsworth (1770-1850)

Larkspur. . . . . .An open heart
Laurel leaves . . . . .Glory, perseverance
Lavender . . . . .Devotion, luck, success, happiness
Lilac. . . . . .Youthful innocence, romance
Linden branches. . . . . . .Romance
Lily, white . . . . .Purity, virginity
Lily, orange. . . . . .Hatred
Lily-of-the-Valley . . . . .Sweetness
Magnolia . . . . .Perseverance, sweetness, love of nature
Marigold . . . . .Remembrance, grief
Marjoram. . . . . .Joy, happiness
Mint. . . . . .Warmth of feeling, protection from illness
Mistletoe . . . . .Fertility
Mock Orange. . . . . . . .Deceit, counterfeit
Morning Glory. . . . . . .Affection
Moss . . . . .Charity
Moss Rose . . . . .I admire you from afar, voluptuous love
Myrtle . . . . .Love, marriage
Narcissus . . . . .Respect, chivalry, regard, egotism

Nasturtium . . . . .Patriotism
Oak leaves . . . . .Heroism, hospitality
Oleander . . . . .Beware
Olive branch . . . . .Peace
Orange blossoms . . . . .Bridal festivities, chastity,
                          fidelity, loving thoughts
Oregano. . . . . .Happiness
Orchid, pink . . . . .Pure affection, beauty
Palm leaves. . . . . .Victory
Pansy . . . . .Good thoughts of you
Parsley . . . . .Merriment
Passionflower . . . . .Faith
Peach blossom . . . . . . .Captive heart
Peony. . . . . .Wedded bliss, aphrodisiac
Peppermint . . . . .Warmth, cordiality

Just now the lilac is in bloom
All before my little room;
And in my flowerbeds I think
Smile the carnation and the pink;
And from the borders, well I know,
The poppy and the pansy blow.

— *Rupert Brooke (1887-1915)*

Petunia. . . . . .Don't despair, your
                          presence soothes me
Phlox . . . . .Proposal of love,
                          agreement
Pine . . . . .Hope
Poppy, red . . . . .Consolation
Plum blossoms . . . . . . .Fidelity
Primrose. . . . . .Youth
Queen Anne's Lace. . . . .Protection
Ranunculus, white . . . . .Overpowering interest in
                          you
Rosa, Centifolia, ...Ambassador of love
  Cabbage Rose
Rose, amethyst . . . . .I will love you forever
Rose, coral . . . . .Longevity, admiration,
                          desire
Rose, cream . . . . .Perfection
Rose, golden. . . . . .Jealousy
Rose, lavender . . . . . . .Rarity, love at first sight
Rose, orange. . . . . .I love you with enthusiasm
Rose, peach . . . . .Immorality, modesty
Rose, pink . . . . .Grace, beauty, youth,
                          innocent love
Rose, red . . . . .I love you, passion (used
                          to mean deep shame)
Rose, rose. . . . . .Pride, shyness

Rose, white.	Silence, keep my secret, beauty and respect, birth	Sweet William	Gallantry
Rose, yellow	Friendship, I love another, joy, jealousy	Tarragon.	Lasting involvement
Rose, white/pink	Two roses of two different colors, unity, commitment	Taxus, Yew	Continued life
		Thistle	Sternness
		Thyme	Courage, strength
Rose, a single	Simplicity, perpetual love	Tuberose.	Dangerous pleasures
Rose bud	Hope, innocence	Tulip	Consuming love, fame, symbol of the rich
Rosemary	Remembrance	Tulip, red	Declaration of love, ardent love
Rudbeckia	Justice		
Sage	Domestic virtue, skill, household, faith, immortality	Tulip, white	Lost love
		Tulip, yellow.	Hopeless love
		Tulip, pink	Love, imagination
Snowdrops	Hope, purity	Tulip, variegated.	Beautiful eyes
Southernwood	Constancy	Verbena	May you get your wish
Spurge	Welcome	Veronica.	Fidelity
Statice	Remembrance, gratitude	Violet.	Modesty, faithfulness
Straw	Agreement	Weeping Willow.	Sorrow and bereavement
Straw, broken	Broken agreement	Wheat	Fertility
Sunflower.	Pride, respect, sunshine	Yarrow	Health, healing
Sweet Basil	Best wishes	Zinnia	Thoughts of an absent friend
Sweet Pea	Delicate pleasures, birth, goodbye		

Heaven is under our feet as well as over our heads.

– Henry David Thoreau (1817-1862)

A Sonnet For My Loved One

The sonnet, a love poem that originated during the Italian Renaissance, means "little song" in Italian. It contains fourteen lines, each comprised of ten syllables. Though this poetic form was first popularized by Shakespeare, both Elizabeth Barrett Browning and Alfred Lord Tennyson were renowned for their sonnets composed during the Victorian era. Following Evelyn Byers' example on the following page, try writing a sonnet for your loved one.

With statues on the terraces and peacocks strutting by; but the glory of the garden lies in more than meets the eye.

– Rudyard Kipling (1865-1936)

Ode To Ray

Our time together is a splendid one
Years spent in sharing warmth and tenderness.
We love and laugh and sing our own sweet songs,
And strive to give each other more, not less.
You'll always be the only love I need
My fiery sun, my glowing moon, my star,
To light my way along life's treacherous road
And walk beside me, though the way be far.
Oh, when we met, I knew you were the one
To be my sweet companion through the years
To stand with me until the time has come
When memories keep us smiling through our tears,
And, dearest one, though we must part someday,
The love we share shall never fade away.

With love,
Linda

Edible Flowers

Edible flowers are far from being a new concept. Traditions of flower cookery come to us from the Victorian era and go back as far as the Roman Empire. I have been using flowers for garnishes and seasonings for some time. They are a very appealing and attractive way to enhance each meal.

Flowers with strong, distinctive fragrances, such as marigold, rose, yarrow, jasmine, and chamomile are good for teas. The flavor and fragrance will be released by steeping one teaspoon of the dried petals in a cup of boiled water for five to ten minutes. I will also add these to my favorite green teas for a healthy tea to sip. I find drinking herbal teas and plenty of fresh water with special (blossom) ice cubes to be very refreshing.

Decorate plain tossed salads with rosemary blossoms, chive blossoms, nasturtiums, or Johnny jump-ups.

Freeze blossoms of rose petals, Johnny-jump-up, or your favorite other blossoms in ice cubes. This adds a distinctive accent to party punches or just plain ice water!

Use rose- or lavender-flavored jams, jellies, and butter to serve with tea.

Decorate the top of fresh cupcakes or iced cake with mildly- flavored fresh flowers like pansies, roses, dianthus, Johnny jump-ups, or calendulas.

Using your own imagination, you will find many creative ways to use edible flowers to add a special taste and beauty to the meals you prepare.

In all things of nature there is something of the marvelous.

– Aristotle (384-322 B.C.)

Common Name	Botanical Name	Comments
Angelica	Angelica archangelica	May cause skin allergies in some individuals. Good on fish, and the stems are especially popular candied. Tastes like celery.
Anise Hyssop	Angastache foeniculum	Tastes sweet; anise-like; licorice taste.
Apple	Malus (Spp.*)	Eat in moderation; may contain cyanide precursors. Has a delicate floral flavor.
Arugula	Eruca vesicaria	Tastes nutty, spicy, peppery.
Basil	Ocimum basilicum	Different varieties have different milder flavors of the corresponding leaves. Tastes like lemon, mint.
Bee Balm	Monarda (Spp.*)	Used in place of bergamot to make a tea with a flavor similar to that of Earl Grey Tea.
Begonia	Begonia X tuberose	**ONLY HYBRIDS** are edible. The flowers and stems contain oxalic acid and should not be consumed by individuals suffering from gout, kidney stones, or rheumatism. Further, the flower should be eaten in strict moderation. Tastes crisp, sour, lemony.
Borage	Borago officinalis	Has a light cucumber flavor.
Burnet	Sanguisorba minor	Has a faint cucumber flavor; very mild.
Calendula	Calendula officinalis	Tastes like "poor man's saffron." Spicy, tangy, peppery; adds a golden hue to foods.
Carnation	Dianthus caryophyllus	Tastes spicy, peppery, clove-like.
Chamomile	Amaemelum nobile	Has a faint apple flavor; good as a tea.
Chicory	Cichorium intybus	Buds may be pickled.
Chives	Allium schoenoprasum	Have a mild onion flavor.
Chives, Garlic	Allium tuberosum	Have a garlicky flavor.

Note: Spp. means that you may eat any variety of this species; they are non-poisonous.

Common Name	Botanical Name	Comments
Chrysanthemum Garland	*Chrysanthemum coronarium*	Has a slight to bitter flavor; pungent.
Citrus, Lemon	*Citrus lemon*	Has a waxy, pronounced flavor; use sparingly as an edible garnish; good for making citrus waters.
Clover	*Trifolium*	Raw flower heads may be difficult to digest.
Cornflower, Bachelor's Button	*Centaurea cynannus*	Tastes sweet to spicy; clove-like.
Dandelion	*Taraxacum officinale*	Very young buds fried in butter taste similar to mushrooms.
Day Lily	*Hemerocallis*	Many lilies (*lilium*) contain alkaloids and are **NOT** edible. Day lilies may act as a laxative. Taste sweet, crunchy, like a crisp lettuce leaf; faintly like chestnuts or beans.
Dill	*Anethum graveolens*	Robust, aromatic; complements sour cream, cheese dips and spreads, seafood.
English Daisy	*Bellis perennis*	Tastes tangy, leafy.

The earth laughs in flowers.

– *Ralph Waldo Emerson (1803-1882)*

Common Name	Botanical Name	Comments
Fennel	*Foeniculum vulgare*	Has a sweet, licorice flavor.
Fuchsia	*Fuchsia X hybrida*	Tastes slightly acidic.
Gardenia	*Gardenia jasminoides*	Has a light, sweet flavor.
Gladiolus	*Gladiolus (Spp. *)*	Taste is similar to that of lettuce.
Hibiscus	*Hibiscus rosasinensis*	Tastes slightly acidic; when boiled makes a nice beverage.
Hollyhock	*Althaea rosea*	Has a very bland, nondescript flavor.
Honeysuckle	*Lonicera japonica*	Berries are highly poisonous. **DO NOT** eat them!
Hyssop	*Hyssopus officinalis*	Should be avoided by pregnant women and by those with hypertension and epilepsy.
Impatiens	*Impatiens wallerana*	Has a very bland, nondescript flavor.

How could such sweet and wholesome hours
Be reckoned but with herbs and flowers?

– Andrew Marvell (1621-1678)

---

* *Note: Spp. means that you may eat any variety of this species; they are non-poisonous.*

Common Name	Botanical Name	Comments
Jasmine, Arabian	*Jasminum sambac*	Has a delicate sweet flavor, used for teas.
Johnny-Jump-Up	*Viola tricolor*	Contains saponins and may be toxic in large amounts; has a sweet to bland flavor.
Lavender	*Lavandula species*	Lavender oil **may be poisonous**. Tastes floral; has a slightly perfumed flavor.
Lemon Verbena	*Aloysia triphylla*	Has a lemony flavor; usually steeped for tea.
Lilac	*Syringa vulgaris*	Tastes lemony, floral, pungent.
Mallow	*Malva sylvestris*	Has a sweet, delicate flavor.
Marigold Signet	*Tagetes tenuifolia* (aka *T. signata*)	Tastes spicy to bitter.
Marjoram	*Origanum majorana*	Slightly minty, citrusy taste; milder than true oregano.
Mint	*Mentha (Spp.*)*	Many flavors from apple to chocolate available.
Mustard	*Brassica (Spp.*)*	Eating this plant in large amounts may cause red blotches.
Nasturtium	*Tropaeolum majus*	Buds are often pickled and used like capers. Tastes sweet, mildly pungent, peppery.
Okra	*Hibiscus esculentus*	Tastes similar to squash blossoms.
Pansy	*Viola X wittrockiana*	Has a very mild sweet to tart flavor.
Pea	*Pisum*	Flowering ornamental sweet peas are **POISONOUS.**
Pineapple Guava	*Feijoa sellowiana*	Tastes similar to the ripe fruit of the plant; flavorful.
Primrose	*Primula vulgaris*	Birdseye Primrose (*P. farinose*) causes contact dermatitis. Has a bland to sweet flavor.
Radish	*Raphanus sativus*	Is a milder, sweeter version of the more familiar radish heat.

Common Name	Botanical Name	Comments
Redbud	*Cercis canadensis*	Tastes mildly sweet.
Rose	*Rosa rugosa* or *R. gallica officinalis*	Has a sweet, aromatic flavor; stronger fragrance produces a stronger flavor. Be sure to remove the bitter white portion of petals.
Rosemary	*Rosmarinus officinalis*	Tastes pine-like, sweet, savory.
Runner Bean	*Phaseolus coccineus*	Tastes like nectar; bean-like.
Safflower	*Carthamus tinctorius*	Another "poor man's saffron" without the pungent aroma or strong flavor of the real thing.
Sage	*Salvia officinalis*	Sage should not be eaten in large amounts over a long period of time. Taste varies by type.
Savory, Summer	*Satureja hortensis*	Lilac flavors are sweet with mild aroma.
Scented Geranium	*Pelargonium*	Citronella variety may not be edible. Taste varies with differing variety, from lemon to mint.
Snapdragon	*Antirrhinum majus*	Tastes bland to bitter.
Society Garlic	*Tulbaghia violacea*	Has a very mild garlic flavor.
Squash Blossom	*Cucurbita pepo (Spp.*)*	Has a sweet, nectar-like flavor.
Sunflower	*Helianthus annus*	Taste is leafy, slightly bitter. Lightly steam petals to lessen bitterness. Unopened flower buds may be steamed like artichoke.
Thyme	*Thymus vulgaris*	Tastes like lemon; has a nice light scent.
Violet	*Viola (Spp.*)*	Tastes sweet, like nectar.
Yucca	*Yucca*	Only the petals are edible. Other parts contain saponin, which is **POISONOUS**. Large amounts May be **HARMFUL**. Is crunchy, with a fresh flavor.

---

* Note: Spp. means that you may eat any variety of this species; they are non-poisonous.

Roses, Roses, Roses For Many Uses

Do not restrict the use of roses in cooking to garnishes only. For a touch of eighteenth century in today's world, add pink petals to your pancake batter, vanilla puddings, or butter cookie dough. An old well-kept secret is to add the reddest rose petals to cherry pie filling. You will be rewarded with divine color.

Surprise your family or friends with rose tea and rose-flavored punch. Freeze the nicest blooms in ice cubes for special drinks or make a rose ice ring to float in the punch.

I enjoy rose jelly and rose butter with fresh breads and hot tea. The rose butter is equally delicious on petite sandwiches. Always keep rose sugar ready to serve on cereals or for tea sweetening.

Rose syrup or rose honey is a nice addition to fruit salads or petite, shaped pancakes. The great thing when using honey is that you receive minerals and vitamins as a bonus.

Note: Always remove the bitter portion of rose petals before using them in recipes.

That which we call a rose
By any other name would
smell as sweet.

– William Shakespeare (1564-1616)
Romeo and Juliet, Act 2, Scene 2

Strawberry Cake with Creamy Rose Frosting

1 box yellow cake mix
1 ½ cups frozen, drained strawberries
2 eggs
½ cup plain yogurt
1 box strawberry Jello®
½ cup water
1 drop of rose geranium oil
2 drops of red food coloring

Preheat oven to 350º. Mix all the ingredients. Pour into a 9"x 13" pan that has been coated with cooking spray. Bake for approximately 35 minutes; allow to cool. Then add icing (see below). Cut into 2"x 4"-long strips for serving. Garnish with rose petals and fresh strawberries for a gorgeous tray of desserts.

Icing
8 ounces cream cheese
1 ½ sticks unsalted butter, at room temperature (do not substitute with margarine)
1 teaspoon vanilla extract
1 drop of rose geranium essential oil
1 tablespoon strawberry juice
1 ½ pounds confectioners sugar

Cream all ingredients (except sugar) until light and fluffy. Slowly add sugar until desired spreading consistency is reached. This frosting may be kept in the refrigerator for up to one week. This cake and icing recipe is also delightful made into cupcakes.

...and blossom as the rose.

– Isaiah 35:1

Rose-Scented Sugar

Choose a pint- size glass container. Fill 1/3 full with sugar or Splenda.® Sprinkle with rose petals. Cover petals with more sugar. Add more rose petals. Seal with a lid; shake. Store in a cool dark place for about three weeks. The flavor of the sugar is enhanced with age. Replenish the sugar as used; it will take on the fragrance of the rose petals. Caution: Never use rose petals that have been sprayed with any type of pesticides.

When rose-scented sugar is added to tea it creates a pleasing, light taste. Serve with a fresh rose lying beside the teacup. This adds a charming touch to a simple tea time.

Strawberry-Rose Butter

1 stick sweet cream butter (do not substitute with margarine)
3 tablespoons strawberry jam
1 drop of rose geranium essential oil
1 teaspoon crushed, dried rose petals

Allow butter to soften. Stir in jam, oil, and rose petals until thoroughly mixed and creamy. Place in glass serving dish. Best when allowed to set 48 hours to enhance flavor.

Edible Sugared Rose

Rose petals
1 egg white at room temperature
Few drops of water
1 cup superfine sugar

Rinse petals; pat dry. Beat the egg white with water in a small bowl until frothy. Using a small paintbrush, coat each petal with the egg-white mixture. Sprinkle sugar evenly on both sides; form petal back into original shape with a toothpick. Place the rose petals on waxed paper. Allow to air-dry 12 to 36 hours or until completely dry. Humid days can affect drying time. You may place in a warm oven (150-200 degrees). Leave the oven door slightly ajar for several hours. You may store these in an air-tight container. They will keep for up to one year. These make beautiful garnishes for many foods.

Creamy Rose Dip

8 ounces cream cheese, at room temperature
1 tablespoon finely-chopped fragrant rose blossoms
4 tablespoons confectioners sugar (or substitute 3 packages artificial sweetener)

Combine all the ingredients, mixing until smooth and creamy. Spoon into small crystal dish. Chill until serving time. Serve with freshly-sliced strawberries, apples, or spread onto your favorite breads.

Note: Always remove the bitter portion of the rose petals before using in recipe.

Enjoy what Mother Nature gives us before Father Time takes it away.

– Unknown

Strawberry-Rose Salads

1 head Bibb lettuce, rinsed and torn
2 Belgian endives, rinsed and torn, to scatter over lettuce
¼ cup pine nuts
(I prefer soft pink or red) petals of 2 mature roses (bitter part removed), and 16 fresh strawberries, rinsed and dried

¼ cup light olive oil
6 tablespoons raspberry vinegar
4 chilled plates

Arrange the lettuce, endive, pine nuts, and rose petals. Place four strawberries on each chilled plate. Whisk the olive oil and vinegar. Drizzle over salad. Serve immediately. Pretty, delicious, and nutritious.

Sweet and Waiting Syrup

3 cups granulated sugar
3 cups cold water

In a saucepan, boil water and sugar until completely clear and all sugar crystals have dissolved. Allow syrup to cool. Place in air-tight container and refrigerate. I use glass jar with lid. The two sweet things about this mixture are that it will keep for months and is ready to use when you need it.

Lemon Scones with Rose Petal Jam

2 cups unbleached all-purpose flour
1 cup cake flour
½ cup granulated sugar plus 2 tablespoons
1 tablespoon plus 1 teaspoon baking powder
½ teaspoon salt
1 large egg, beaten
1 cup heavy cream plus 1 tablespoon
1 teaspoon grated lemon zest
Devonshire cream

Preheat oven to 450 degrees F. Line baking sheet with parchment paper. Combine flours, ½ cup sugar, baking powder, and salt in mixing bowl. Stir in egg, cream, and lemon zest into dry ingredients just to moisten. Turn dough out onto lightly- floured work surface and divide in half. Shape each half into a 6-inch disk. With sharp knife, cut each disk into 6 wedges. Place wedges ½-inch apart on baking sheet. Brush tops with cream and sprinkle with granulated sugar. Bake until golden, 12 to 15 minutes. Remove from oven and cool.

Yields: 12 scones.

Note: Serve with Rose Petal Jam and Devonshire cream.

Rose Petal Jam

2 pounds strawberries, washed and hulled
½ cup fresh rose petals, pesticide free, washed
2 tablespoons fresh lemon juice
2 pounds granulated sugar

Place berries in heavy, non-reactive deep preserving pan. Mash lightly and bring to boil. Cut off the hearts of the rose petals, as they are bitter. When the berries are translucent, add rose petals, lemon juice, and sugar. Boil rapidly until jam reaches the setting stage, 214 degrees F. on jelly thermometer.

Ladle into sterilized jars. Top off with melted paraffin and seal with lids.

Yields: 4 half-pints

It is the month of June.
The month of leaves and roses
When pleasant sights salute the eyes
And pleasant scents the noses.

– *Nathaniel Parker Willis (1806-1867)*

Rose Petal Scones

2¼ cups all-purpose flour
2 teaspoons sugar
¾ teaspoon salt
2 teaspoons baking powder
½ teaspoon baking soda
½ teaspoon cinnamon
4 tablespoons unsalted butter
1 cup heavy cream
1 tablespoon. rose water
2 tablespoons edible rose petals, cleaned and finely
    shredded

Icing:

1 cup confectioners sugar
1 tablespoon plum jelly
2 teaspoons rose water

Preheat oven to 425 degrees.
In a large bowl, combine the flour, sugar, salt, baking powder, baking soda, and cinnamon. Cut in the butter and mix until coarse crumbs form. In a separate bowl, combine the cream and the rose water. Stir in the shredded rose petals. Add the cream-rose mixture to the dry ingredients, stirring until a soft dough forms. Drop by teaspoonsful onto an ungreased cookie sheet. Bake for 10-12 minutes or until golden brown.

Prepare the icing:

In a small bowl, combine the powdered sugar, rose water, and the plum jelly. Beat until smooth. Add another teaspoon of rose water if the icing is too thick. Drizzle over warm scones. Arrange on platter and garnish with fresh roses. Sprinkle with shredded rose petals.

Raspberry Rose Soup

1 quart fresh or frozen raspberries
Juice of a quarter of a lemon
1 cinnamon stick
3 cups water
1/3 cup sugar
¼ teaspoon salt
2 tablespoons cornstarch
¾ cup heavy cream

In a saucepan, combine the berries, lemon juice, cinnamon stick, water, sugar, and salt; bring to a boil. Simmer for 7 minutes. Make a paste of cornstarch and a little water; add to the soup. Stir and cook for 1 minute. Remove cinnamon stick and force remaining mixture through a sieve. Stir in the cream and chill well. Serve in chilled bowls or cup. Garnish with fresh mint leaves and raspberries.

Rose Petal Punch and Blooming Tea

Blooming white tea*
Bigelow® Green tea
Pear juice
1 quart strawberry soda
1 quart fresh strawberries
1 large rose blossom (red or pink with no pesticide sprays)
Rose water
Red food coloring

Steep Blooming white tea (make 12 cups); add ¾ cup Sweet and Waiting Syrup, page 51. Steep green tea (make 6 cups); add ½ cup Sweet and Waiting Syrup, page 51. Place in refrigerator; chill until serving time. Chill strawberry soda.

Blend 2 cups strawberries with 2 cups rose water and pour into a ring mold. Freeze the day before serving punch.

When ready to serve, blend 3 cups pear juice with 1 cup fresh strawberries. Place in punch bowl; add all other ingredients: Blooming white tea, green tea, frozen ring, cold strawberry soda, and 2 drops of red food coloring. Float rose petals/whole strawberries on top of prepared punch.

Variation: For orange punch, substitute strawberry soda with orange soda, 1 quart fresh strawberries with 1 quart orange sherbet, and red rose blossoms with white or apricot-colored roses. Omit red food coloring. Substitute 2 cups fresh strawberries with orange sherbet (softened). Slice 2 large navel oranges and place in the bottom of the ring mold. Cover orange slices with 1 quart softened orange sherbet. Return to freezer and place in punch bowl when ready to serve. Add remaining ingredients.

Blooming white tea and green tea are both very high in antioxidants. Their bulbs unfold before your eyes into a dazzling water garden, producing the most soothing, delightful, and flavorful teas.

*Blooming white tea may be purchased on my website: www.lindajhawkins.com

Fairy Tea Sandwiches

Cake:
1 tablespoon unsalted butter
2 cups all-purpose flour
2 teaspoons baking powder
¼ teaspoon salt
3 large eggs
8 ounces unsalted butter, melted
1½ cups granulated sugar
1 teaspoon vanilla extract
2/3 cup milk

Filling:
4 ounces hazelnut spread
2 ounces cream cheese, softened
¼ cup fresh raspberries

Preheat oven to 350 degrees. Grease a 9"x 5"x 3" loaf pan with unsalted butter and line bottom with parchment paper. Sift flour, baking powder, and salt onto waxed paper and set aside.

Using electric mixer, beat eggs until fluffy and light; add sugar, beating as you go. Slowly add butter and mix. Add vanilla. With mixer at low speed, add a third of the dry ingredients; add half the milk. Add a third of the dry ingredients and mix. Add remaining milk and dry ingredients, mixing. Pour batter into pan and bake until cake springs back from sides of pan when touched, 35 to 40 minutes. Remove from oven and cool in pan for 10 minutes. Take cake from pan and cool thoroughly on wire rack.

With electric knife, slice cake into ¼-inch slices. Spread hazelnut spread on one slice and place a second cake slice on top.

Blend cream cheese and raspberries in food processor. Spread on another slice of cake and place on top of the first two slices. Remove crusts. Cut each sandwich into ½-inch fingers. Place on sides so stripes of hazelnut and raspberry filling show. These are light in appearance and will disappear immediately.

Yields: 4 dozen.

Strawberry Lavender Jam

1 pound strawberries
2 pounds sugar
¼ cup lavender tea
Juice of 4 lemons

Place strawberries that have been washed, dried, and hulled in a large bowl with the sugar and ¼ cup lavender tea. Set in refrigerator overnight. Place the berry mixture in a large non-aluminum saucepan. Add the lemon juice. Cook over medium heat until the mixture comes to a boil, then continue to cook for 20 to 25 minutes. Skim any foam from the top. Pour into sterilized jars, leaving ¼-inch head-space. Apply lids that have been treated according to manufacturer's directions. Process in a simmering hot water bath at 190 to 200 degrees for 10 minutes.

I must own that I would do almost anything, and grow almost anything, for the sake of fragrance.

– Reginald Farrer (1880-1920)

Daring Delightful Chocolate

1 box brownie mix with chocolate chips
1 large box instant chocolate pudding
1 large container of Cool Whip®
1 bag of Heath Bits®

Bake brownies according to package directions. Allow to cool completely; crumble into small pieces. Prepare pudding according to package directions. Layer the ingredients in order listed. You may place in a 9"x13" pan; allow to set 2 or more hours. Cut into squares, garnish, and serve. This recipe is very attractive when layered in parfait or pelfmeiser glasses. Top with chocolate leaves and nice fresh flowers.

Floral Butter

Use fresh blossoms from plants such as roses, petunias, pansies, carnations, rosemary, thyme, oregano, or sage. Use only pesticide-free, edible flowers.

½ pound unsalted butter, at room temperature
1½ tablespoons minced fresh mint
¼ teaspoon.lemon zest
1 tablespoon fruit preserves (your choice)
1 teaspoon rose water
1 tablespoon chopped pecans

Rinse flowers; pat dry between paper towels. Set aside. Combine butter, mint, lemon zest, preserves, rose water, and pecans in food processor until smooth and soft. Add petals from one blossom; continue to process until finely chopped with butter mixture. Place remaining blossoms in bottom of small, decorative glass dish; use butter to hold blossoms in place. Decorate top with more blossoms. Cover and chill for 2 or 3 days, allowing butter to absorb flowers' sweet flavor. Serve with muffins, scones, or bread.

Rose Raspberry Butter

1 stick sweet cream butter (no margarine)
3 tablespoons raspberry preserves
2 tablespoons dried rose petals.

Allow butter to soften at room temperature. Stir preserves and rose petals into butter. Place in covered dish to serve over hot biscuits.

Nasturtium Baskets

Filling ingredients:
4 cups cooked brown rice
1 cup diced carrots, blanched
2 cups frozen baby peas, blanched
½ cup chopped green onion
1 cup mayonnaise
1 cup lemon yogurt
Salt and pepper to taste

Combine all ingredients and refrigerate until ready to use.

Wrapping ingredients:
30 large nasturtium leaves
30 whole chives

Dip nasturtium leaves in hot water and pat dry. Turn leaves stem side up. Place a small melon scoop portion of rice mixture on each leaf. Pull two sides of the leaf up like a basket. Tie with a single long chive. Clip ends if they are too long. Top each by adding a nasturtium bloom.

Special Applesauce

48 ounces sugar-free applesauce
1 teaspoon. apple pie spice
25 packets Splenda®
½ teaspoon. ground cloves
1 teaspoon cinnamon
1/2 cup sugar-free apple juice*

Mix all ingredients; refrigerate up to 14 days. Use sauce for apple cake or pie, served over pancakes, on hot buttered biscuits, over vanilla ice cream, or enjoy alone.

You may leave juice out for a thicker sauce or use water as juice replacement.

Daring Delightful Chocolate

Coconut Pound Cake with Glaze

2 cups sugar
2 cups flour
1 cup butter
1 ½ teaspoons baking powder
5 eggs
1 cup buttermilk
1 small can shredded coconut
1 teaspoon coconut extract

Cream sugar and butter. Add eggs, one at a time. Sift flour and baking powder. Add buttermilk. Fold in coconut and coconut extract last. Bake 1 hour at 350º in tube pan. This is a super- moist, heavy cake.

Glaze:
1 cup sugar
1 teaspoon coconut extract
½ cup water

Boil sugar and water for 1 minute. Add coconut extract. Pour over cake while hot; let cool in tube pan. Remove cake when completely cool. Garnish with mint sprig and lemon slices.

Dressed Eggs

8 eggs

Boil for 15 minutes; pour off hot water and cover with cold water. Allow to sit 10 minutes.
Peel off outer shell; cut eggs in half and remove yolks.

Mix all yolks with:
¼ cup salad dressing
½ teaspoon prepared mustard
salt and pepper to taste
2 teaspoons sweet pickle relish or 2 teaspoons chopped pimentos (optional)

Spoon filling back into egg whites.
Garnish with paprika, parsley flakes, sliced olives, or lovely flower blossoms.

Kentucky Derby Pie

½ cup butter, melted
1 cup sugar
4 eggs, beaten
1/8 teaspoon salt
1 teaspoon vanilla
1 cup light corn syrup
½ cup chocolate chips
1 cup broken pecan pieces
1 9-inch, deep-dish pie crust

Mix first six ingredients together until well blended. Add pecans and chocolate chips. Pour into unbaked pie shell and bake in 350° oven for 40-50 minutes.

Allow pie to cool. Place chocolate rose leaves around edges. To make leaves: Brush the undersides of fresh rose leaves with melted chocolate (use small brush). Chill until firm. Gently peel the leaves from the chocolate when ready.

Clean and round, heavy and sound, inside a bulb a flower is found.

– Anonymous

Never-Fail Pie Crust

1 cup shortening
½ cup boiling water

Whip together until creamy; allow time to cool.

Sift together 3 cups self-rising flour and ½ teaspoon of sugar; add to shortening. Mix thoroughly. This is enough dough to make four pie crusts. Sprinkle counter surface with flour; place ¼ of dough on surface. Roll out with a rolling-pin; press gently into glass pie plate and flute edges of crust. Fill and bake at 350 degrees for 12-15 minutes, until brown.

Pineapple/Lemon-Lime Crunch

1 small package each of lemon and lime Jello®
1 20 ounce can crushed pineapple packed in its own juice – drain juice and set aside.
2 cups hot water
2 8-ounce packages cream cheese
½ cup chopped pecans

Mix water, and Jello® together. Beat in softened cream cheese. Add pineapple juice. Refrigerate until syrupy. Add crushed pineapple and stir. Put into 9"x 11" pan. Refrigerate. Sprinkle layer of pecans on top. When mixture is set firm, cut into squares and garnish plate with rose blooms or mint leaves.

If you could paint one autumn leaf, you could paint the world.

– John Ruskin (1819-1900)

And 'tis my faith, that every flower enjoys the air it breathes.

– William Wordsworth (1770-1850)

Green Bars with Cream Cheese Frosting

2 cups sugar
1 cup oil
3 eggs
2 cups flour
1 teaspoon baking powder
2 teaspoons baking soda
1 teaspoon salt
2 cups shredded zucchini
1 cup chopped nuts

Cream the sugar, oil, and eggs. In another bowl, mix all dry ingredients and add to the creamed mixture. Add nuts and zucchini. Mix and pour out onto a greased cookie sheet, or into a cake pan for a cake. Bake at 350º for 30 to 35 minutes. Let cool. Children love the color green, and they love this recipe. Just don't reveal the ingredients. Another healthy option is adding ½ cup raisins.

Cream Cheese Frosting:
½ stick butter
3 ounces cream cheese
½ teaspoon vanilla
2 cups confectioners sugar
1 ½ teaspoons milk

Mix all together and spread over cake, or cut into bars and serve. Decorate with mint leaves and flower blossoms.

Pleasing Biscuits

2 ¾ cups self-rising flour
½ cup canola oil
1 cup buttermilk

Preheat oven to 400º. Mix dough. Sprinkle counter-top with flour and roll dough out to 1 ½-inch thickness. Use any shape metal cookie cutters to cut biscuits, placing into oiled pan. Coat top of biscuits by turning over in pan. This allows tops to brown nicely. Bake until golden brown, approximately 15-20 minutes. If you choose to bake mini- biscuits, cut cooking time. Serve with your favorite flavored butter.

Mini Tart Crust

1 cup flour
3 ounces cream cheese
1 stick butter

To make tarts, mix all ingredients together to make pastry. Chill. Form little tarts in tart pan. Bake at 350º for 12-15 minutes. Fill with fresh fruit, or any favorite pie filling. These are great with any cream or fruit filling.

Rainbow Spiced Mini Corn Muffins

¼ cup plain, fat-free yogurt
1 cup buttermilk
2 cups corn meal
¼ cup shredded cheddar cheese
½ cup- self rising flour
1 egg
2 packets Splenda® or 1 tablespoon sugar
2 jalapeno peppers, chopped
2 tablespoons chopped pimentos

Preheat oven to 425º. Spray mini-muffin tin. Add mixture, filling two-thirds full. Bake for 12-15 minutes until golden brown. Remove from oven, and serve hot with butter. These are wonderful served with the Rainbow Spiced Corn Chowder (below).

Rainbow Spiced Corn Chowder

3 cups loose-pack frozen whole kernel corn
1 to 2 fresh jalapeno peppers, chopped
1 ½ cups chicken broth
2- ounce jar diced pimentos
1 cup milk or light cream
½ cup Velveeta® cheese or crumbled feta cheese

In blender, place 1 ½ cups corn and broth; blend until smooth. In saucepan, mix all ingredients, cook for 15 minutes, and top each serving with chive or green onion tops.

Benedictine Tea Sandwiches

"Miss Jenny" Benedict was born in the 1880s near Harrod's Creek, Kentucky, near Louisville. After attending a local public school she went to the Boston Cooking School and studied under the famous chef Fannie Farmer. In 1893, "Miss Jenny" opened her first confectionery, where she made candied roses, cakes, and as much as 300 pounds of spun sugar ribbons at a time. But it was her party sandwiches made with a cucumber spread that brought her fame. "Miss Jenny" was the first woman in the South to hold a Board of Trade membership. She authored a recipe book titled *The Blue Ribbon Cook Book* and her autobiography, *The Road to Dream Acre*.

Benedictine:
12 ounces cream cheese, softened
1 medium cucumber, seeded
1 green onion
1 teaspoon salt
1 drop Tabasco® sauce
½ cup mayonnaise
Fresh lemon juice

Chop cucumber in food processor until fine and drain off juice. Add green onion and process until fine; add cream cheese, salt, and mayonnaise; blend. Add lemon juice to spreading consistency and Tabasco® to taste. Refrigerate until use, but let it soften before spreading.

Pimento Cheese:
12 ounces sharp cheddar cheese, shredded.
Mayonnaise
Jar of pimentos

Process cheese in food processor, adding just enough mayonnaise to moisten (3 to 4 tablespoons). Add half jar of pimentos; process until they disappear. Stir in the rest of pimentos. Refrigerate.

To make one Tea Sandwich:
Spread Benedictine and Pimento Cheese on two slices of your choice of bread. Place Pimento Cheese slice on bottom and Benedictine on top, with spreads facing up. Using large open biscuit cutter or cookie cutter, cut through both slices. Garnish with halved cherry tomato and parsley.

Oh, what a goodly and glorious show!
The stately trees have decked themselves with white,
And stand transfigured in a robe of light;
Wearing for each lost leaf a flake of snow.

– Richard Wilton, Old Farmer's Almanac (1903)

Hot Brown Quiche

Since Louisville, Kentucky, is the home of the "Hot Brown." I developed this version for *Somewhere in Thyme*. It quickly became one of the customers' favorites. We made ours in jumbo muffin tins without a crust, but this recipe may be made in two 9-inch deep-dish pie plates, with or without the crust.

1 24-ounce container cottage cheese
1 24- ounce container sour cream
6 large eggs
6 tablespoons flour
3 cups shredded cheddar cheese
2 cups roasted turkey breast, cubed
1/2 cup fried bacon, crumbled

In a large mixing bowl, blend together cottage cheese and sour cream. Add eggs one at a time alternately with the flour. Fold in the cheese, turkey, and bacon. Pour mixture into greased and floured tins or pie crusts. Bake in 350 degree oven until center is firm, approximately 1 hour.

Mornay Sauce
1/3 cup butter
1/3 cup flour
3 cups milk
1 teaspoon salt
¼ teaspoon pepper
1 egg, well beaten
1 cup shredded sharp cheddar cheese

Melt butter in saucepan; add flour and whisk well while cooking on low for 3 minutes. Slowly whisk in milk and cook until it thickens; add salt and pepper. Add a bit of sauce to the beaten egg until melted. Serve over Hot Brown Quiche. Slice and garnish with tomato slices and bacon bits.

Mint Julep Punch
(Non-Alcoholic Version)

5 cups boiling water
5 mint tea bags
1 cup sugar
1 12-ounce can frozen orange juice, undiluted
1 12-ounce can frozen lemonade, undiluted

Pour boiling water over tea bags; steep 5 minutes. Stir in sugar, and steep 5 more minutes. Remove tea bags; pour tea into 4 -quart pitcher or punch bowl. Stir in juice concentrates and 7 cups ice cold water. Serve over ice with mint sprigs and fruit slices.

Lemon Raspberry Bars

1 ¾ cups flour 4 large eggs
1 1/3 cups granulated sugar
2/3 cup confectioners sugar 3 tablespoons flour
1/4 cup cornstarch 4 lemons, juice and zest
1 ½ sticks butter, cold (12 tablespoons)
1/3 cup half-and-half

Heat oven to 350 degrees. Mix flour, sugar, and corn-starch together. Cut in butter with a food processor or by hand until mixture looks like coarse crumbs. Sprinkle mixture into a 13"x 9" baking dish. Press firmly with fingers to cover bottom of pan evenly and ½ inch up sides of pan. Chill prepared crust for 30 minutes while you make filling. Bake unfilled crust for 20 minutes on middle rack. Meanwhile, beat eggs lightly; add sugar and flour and beat together. Stir in lemon juice, zest, and milk, and blend well. Reduce oven temperature to 325 degrees and pour lemon mixture on crust while it is still warm. Bake for 20 minutes or until filling is firm. Cool on wire rack at least 30 minutes before cutting (pizza cutter works well). Sieve confectioners sugar on lemon bars just before serving. Garnish each bar with a fresh rasp-berry and a sprig of mint. Yummy!

There is enough in a single flower for the ornament of a score of cathedrals.

— John Ruskin (1819-1900)

Chocolate Cherry Scones

1 egg, lightly beaten
2 cups flour
1 teaspoon vanilla
1/3 cup sugar
1/3 cup half- and- half
1/3 cup cocoa
1 cup white chocolate chips
1 tablespoon baking powder
½ cup dried cherries or cranberries
½ teaspoon salt
Coarse sanding sugar
½ cup cold butter (1 stick)

Heat oven to 400 degrees. Combine flour, sugar, co-coa, baking powder, and salt in large bowl; cut in butter until mixture looks like coarse crumbs. Stir in mixture of egg, vanilla, and cream, just until moist-ened. Add chips and cherries and turn dough onto lightly-floured surface. Pat gently until dough is about an inch thick (remember, the less you handle the dough, the lighter your scones will be).

Cut out scones with a biscuit cutter, being careful to lift cutter straight up; don't twist. Dip cutter in sand-ing sugar for easier release. Bake on ungreased baking sheet for about 10 minutes. Pull out just before done and allow to cool on pan for 5 minutes. Best served warm with cold clotted cream.

Cucumber Crab Tea Sandwiches

½ pound fresh lump crab meat
1 8-ounce package cream cheese, softened
½ teaspoon minced garlic
1 teaspoon Worcestershire Sauce®
1 teaspoon fresh chives
1 teaspoon fresh parsley
1½ teaspoons Old Bay® seasoning
1 English cucumber or large garden variety
Fresh dill

Drain crab meat; remove any bits of shell. Mix cream cheese and next 5 ingredients in food processor until smooth. Stir in crab meat. Cover and chill at least 8 hours. Spread on baguette slices; decorate tops with cucumber curls (thin slices of cucumber curled with a knife) and fresh dill. Or, cut ends off a large garden cucumber. Cut cucumber in half lengthwise. Hollow out each piece, removing seeds. Cut cucumbers into 2" thick slices, making semi-circles. Shave off a little from the bottom of each so that they won't fall over when filled. Fill with crab mixture, and garnish with dill; place upright on a plate lined with lettuce.

Sun-Dried Tomato Pâté

½ cup sun-dried tomatoes
1 8-ounce package cream cheese
¼ cup butter (½ stick)
½ cup grated fresh parmesan cheese
½ teaspoon minced garlic
½ teaspoon fresh basil
½ teaspoon fresh rosemary

Combine all ingredients in a food processor and blend well. Chill at least 4 hours before serving. This recipe makes 1 ½ cups. Double the batch so you won't run out. It will keep in the refrigerator for several weeks. Serve with toast or crackers.

*To see the world in a grain
of sand
And heaven in a wildflower;
Hold infinity in the palm of
your hand
And eternity in an hour.*

– William Blake (1757-1827)

Cheese Crackers

½ pound butter (2 sticks)
2 ½ cups flour
1 pound grated cheddar cheese
Dash of garlic salt

Cream together butter and cheese. Add flour and salt. Roll into tubes of wax paper. Chill several hours until firm enough to slice. Bake at 400 degrees on ungreased baking sheet for about 12 minutes or until just lightly browned.

*Look deep, deep into nature,
and then you will understand
everything better.*

– Albert Einstein (1879-1955)

Yucca Blossom Chicken Salad

1 Boneless, skinless chicken breast, cooked, chopped
   and cooled (or 10 ounces canned chicken)
¼ cup mayonniase
2 tablespoons finely chopped fresh celery
2/3 cup purple seedless grapes, sliced
¼ cup chopped pecans
salt and pepper to taste

Combine all ingredients and refrigerate until ready
to serve.

Prepare yucca blossoms by rinsing gently in cool to
cold water, turn upside down to drain on paper towels. Snip the center of each flower and discard. Place
chilled chicken salad into each blossom before serving. May be served on a bed of lettuce or asparagus
fern leaves.

Quick-Serve Basil Tomatoes

Roma tomatoes, sliced
Soft baby Mozzarella cheese
Olive oil
Fresh basil, rinsed and torn into small pieces

Place tomatoes on serving tray, alternating with
cheese until tray is covered. Sprinkle fresh basil over
top and lightly drizzle with olive oil. May be served
at room temperature or chilled. Garnish center with
sprig of basil or fresh edible flowers.

Yucca Blossom Chicken Salad

Coconut Cake with Lemon Curd Filling

Preheat oven to 350 degrees.

Basic Butter Cake (Double this recipe to get 3 layers; use extra batter to make cupcakes)
3 cups all-purpose flour
3 tablespoons baking powder
¼ teaspoon salt
¾ cup butter
1 ½ cups sugar
1 cup milk
1 teaspoon vanilla
3 egg whites, beaten until stiff

Sift flour, baking powder, and salt into bowl; set aside. Cream butter and sugar until light, 3-4 minutes. Alternate adding flour mixture and milk, beginning and ending with flour. Stir in vanilla. Fold in egg whites gently.

Bake in greased and floured 9" pans for approximately 30 minutes.

Cool ten minutes in pan, then remove and cool completely on wire racks.

Lemon Curd
5 egg yolks
1 cup sugar
4 lemons, zest and juice removed
1 stick butter, cut into pats and chilled

Add about 1 inch of water in medium-sized saucepan. Bring to simmer over medium-high heat. Meanwhile, combine egg yolks and sugar in metal bowl and beat until smooth, about 1 minute. Measure lemon juice, and if needed, add enough cold water to make 1 cup. Add juice and zest to egg mixture and beat until smooth. Once water reaches a simmer, reduce heat to low and place metal bowl on top of saucepan. (Top bowl should not touch the water below). Beat until thickened, about 8 minutes, or until mixture is light yellow and coats the back of a spoon. Remove from heat and add 1 pat of butter at a time, allowing each pat to melt before adding the next one. Pour curd into clean glass bowl and place plastic wrap directly on top of warm curd.

Refrigerate up to 2 weeks.

Butter Cream Frosting
½ cup butter
½ cup Crisco®
2-pound bag confectioners sugar
5-6 tablespoons milk
1 tablespoon vanilla
1 teaspoon meringue powder (optional)

Cream butter and Crisco® 2-3 minutes; add vanilla and 3 tablespoons milk. Gradually add sugar and additional milk as needed, until at spreading consistency. Add meringue powder and beat well for 1 minute. Frosting should be thick but easy to spread. Extra frosting may be stored in refrigerator up to 2 weeks; great on graham crackers!

...I know a little garden-close
set thick with lily and red rose.
Where I would wander if I might
From dewy dawn to dewy night...

– William Morris (1834-1896)

66

Cake Assembly

Make sure cake layers are level; trim as needed. Place first layer on cake plate. Pipe a ring of frosting around the outer edge (this prevents the curd from oozing out). Spread about ½ cup lemon curd onto cake; repeat for second layer. Add top layer of cake, then frost entire outer portion of cake. Before the frosting sets, coat entire cake surface with coconut. Use your hands to coat the sides of the cake – it's messy, but worth the clean-up time!

Time-Saving Version (still delicious!)

Use 2 yellow or French vanilla cake mixes for cake. Purchase lemon curd at specialty kitchen shops. The butter cream is still a must, though, for the home-made touch!

*This we know, the earth
does not belong to man,
man belongs to the earth.*

– *Chief Seattle (1786-1866)*

Adsmore Museum

The Adsmore Museums served as the location of photo shoots for *The Unspoken Language of Fan & Flowers with Recipes.*

Victorian-era costumed guides invite you to step back in time as you enter Adsmore, the beautifully restored home of the prominent Smith-Garrett family. This circa 1857 house is filled with the family's personal belongings—elegant china and crystal, beautiful gowns and linens, and fine antique furniture. Eight yearly settings, revolving around important events in the Smith-Garretts' lives, bring the house alive during your tour.

Learn about Selina Smith's seventy-day Grand Tour and the astonishing news she has for her family upon her return. Slip inside and see the final preparations being made for Selina's wedding to Dr. John Osborne, former Governor of Wyoming, or come and learn about the farmers' rebellion, known as the Black Patch Tobacco War. The Victorian Christmas setting ends the year on a resplendent note.

Also on the grounds for your enjoyment is a restored 1840s log building, where the story of Princeton's first gunsmith is told, and the Carriage Shop, filled with beautiful items for your shopping pleasure.

Tour information and special events offered throughout the year are posted on our website at www.adsmore.org. Come and enjoy the past at Adsmore House and Gardens.

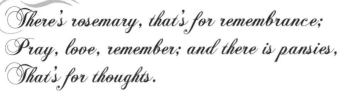

There's rosemary, that's for remembrance;
Pray, love, remember; and there is pansies,
That's for thoughts.

— William Shakespeare (1564-1616)

Hamlet, Act IV, Scene 5, Line 174

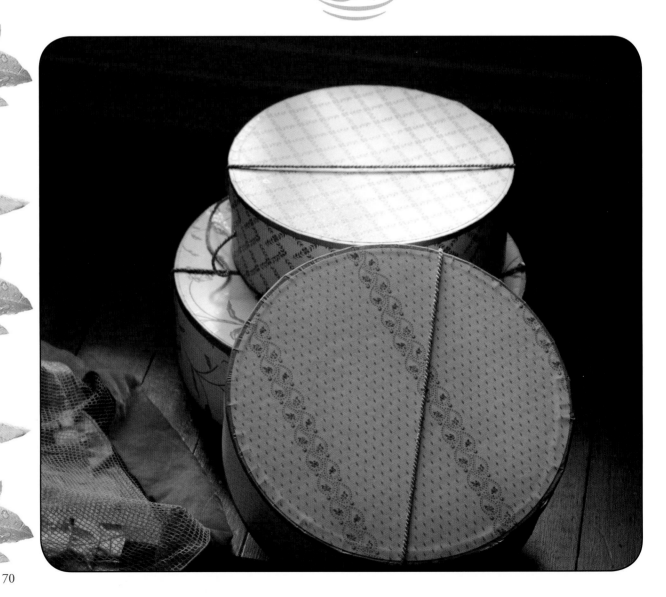

Acknowledgments

To God Be the Glory…

for the many hours of inspiration and fun as I researched the information for this new project. The older I get, the more I enjoy reaching back into the past, trying to pull the best into this present time. Our society today sets a destructive pattern for children from elementary school on, and it only intensifies as they progress through high school, college, and into a career. That destructive pattern is rushing, as elementary students hurry through lunch, taking no thought for relaxing, etiquette, and good communication skills. They must swallow their food quickly, talk to friends with mouths full, then dash off to class.

As an elementary school teacher, I fell into the same "rush" pattern. Today and almost every day, I have to consciously tell myself: Relax, slow down! I feel such peace and satisfaction when I heed my own words.

My pastor, the Reverend Paul Uzzle, Jr., was the greatest motivator in helping me to stop and recognize the rush destructive pattern within myself. I felt I had to be multi-tasking in all areas of my life at all times or I wasn't accomplishing enough. He has often reminded me of how our Master pulled himself away from the crowd to spend quality time alone.

Fix yourself a cup of tea – relax and enjoy life's many blessings; let us break the habit of rushing.

A special thanks to all who have helped make this project fun and successful: Barbara Yonts for the exceptional photography, Admore Museum, and those who shared their recipes – Dolores Snyder, Faye Davidson, Kathy Thiessen, and Rita Joest.

Thanks to the models for their time and dedication to this project: Andrew G., Angela G., Cassidy G., Claire Y., Emily H., Heather U., and Travis U. Thanks to Bonnie Jean Fashions of New York for providing the children's wardrobe (www.bonniejean. com). Thanks to Corner Fashions' Kathy Turley for making this possible.

Thanks to the two Master Gardeners for help and support. As we walked through the floral gardens, they taught me the meanings of the blossoms: Barbara Blanton (artist, Master Gardener), Karen Angelucci (Master Gardener), author of *Secrets of a Kentucky Gardener*, and *Secrets of Tennessee Gardening*, e-mail: mkangelucci@msn.com

Thanks to two avid gardeners for the many cuttings they shared of herbs and flowers to create the old-fashioned tussie-mussies: Brenda Longhofer and Shelia Phelps. Thanks to Jo Stinson, a friend, for helping to get all the flowers arranged for shoots. She is also author of *Right Outside These Walls*. Website: www. JoStinson.com

Thanks to Librarian Kenna Martin for helping with the research from conception to completion. Thanks to typists Regina Hawkins and Samantha Grubb for always getting the rewrites and edits completed with a smile. Thanks to my dear husband Ray. May the next thirty-five years be as good as the first thirty-five. I truly appreciate everyone's contributions; they have made this such a fun project.

71

Recipe Resources

'Tis the last rose of summer; left blooming alone;
All her lovely companions are faded and gone.

— Thomas Moore (1478-1535)